When It's All Said and Done

I'm

Still

Standing

A Woman Overcoming Her Abusive Relationship

AZALEA M. LINDSEY

When It's All Said and Done I'm Still Standing
A Woman Overcoming Her Abusive Relationship

ISBN (Paperback): 979-8-89672-145-1
ISBN (Ebook): 979-8-89672-146-8

PROMINENT
BOOKS

5830 E 2nd St, Ste 7000 #9983
Casper, WY 82609
USA

About the Author

A Louisiana native, Azalea M. Lindsey is the daughter of Willie G. Pope and Odessa Campbell Pope. She was inspired by angels of God and predestined from her mother's womb to be the author of this phenomenal book. Her goal is to lead and link up with every sister on this side of the equator in hopes of taking a stand for women and womanhood. She aims to bring about a solution to some of the contemporary problems that arise from misunderstood relationships and men's delusional conceptions about women. Lindsey hopes to bring about a productive change in the hearts of men all over the world by demonstrating unity and love for mankind and by supporting and accepting some of the flaws and some of the pain that women share. Lindsey is looking forward to bringing readers more motivational, inspirational, and enthusiastic books. She is doing what God has commanded her to do: be fruitful and multiply so men and women all over the world will join in and take her hand while she takes almighty God's hand, which leads us to the promised land of milk and honey.

Contents

Introduction

Imagine being a very attractive young black woman, very well-proportioned, and educated in America—a land that's controlled predominantly by men whose views about relationships are different from women's. A man seems to use women as chess pieces for their own thirsty, blood-sucking gratification.

Now, not all men are this way, but some are. I had to learn that the hard way. Their are some men who know how to treat, respect, admire, and motivate a woman from head to toe. These are the types of men all women should hope to have an encounter with, but it doesn't always turn out this way. Most of us women have to go through some pain. (No pain, no game.)

Let me share my story with you. My name is Deja. I was born in a family of three children. I always knew that I was a very different and peculiar person. I always knew that I didn't fit in with things that weren't godly. I was always the one in my family who watched over everyone and was able to discern where other people were coming from. Even though I didn't always understand, I knew that God had a purpose here on earth for me. Now, my walk hasn't been easy and perfect. I've made so many mistakes in my life because of my disobedience. That's why I look at all of God's beautiful queens who seem to be going in the wrong directions and hope that I can be of encouragement and touch their lives.

Now, getting back to being disobedient—meaning just wanting to do things my own way and not God's way: I have been paying for it ever since. But I do now realize that it's Gods way and not my way. My mother used to always tell me, "Girl, you are so stubborn and hardheaded that it's going to get you know where in life but heart aches and pain." And as I've been here on earth, I've been seeing and feeling every bit of what my mother was telling me, but I just had to do it my way. That's why, with God's help, I'm writing this book and hoping to get the attention of young women so they won't make the same mistakes I did in life by taking the wrong way instead of the right way. There was a saying when I was a child: Why would you want to take the long road in life when you can take the shorter road and be on track? I didn't know or understand what that meant then but now I do. Maybe I just wanted the attention from the opposite sex.

Chapter 1

A Star of Illusions

This is how it happened. One evening, up drove a black Mercedes and out stepped a clean-cut man dressed to impress. Everything seemed like it was neatly made for him. His clothes lay on his back as he turned left to right. I could see how his muscles were just obeying the fabric of his clothes. Even his car seemed like it had respect for him. As he got out, he seemed to have a certain air about himself. He seemed to have the presence of a terrestrial and celestial being from the heavenly body following him. As our eyes met, it was like looking into the universe. A powerful attraction of stars formed to create the attention that I definitely yearned for in a man for my soul.

Now ladies, if a man stepped into the universe looking so divine and well put together, you know that you would want to be a part of his world. But back to the story. I waited to see what move to make before I spoke. At that time I became unaware of my surroundings. He said with a polite, intriguing voice, hello my name is Burt, "May I give you my card?" So I took his card as I shivered because of the chill of the day. Then he said, "Do you need a ride as well?" Well! Hell, I knew I was cold just getting off my nine-to-five job. Accepting a ride and receiving his card wasn't going to cost me anything so I said cheerfully yes. But I told him that I lived a couple of miles away so I asked if that would be problem for him.

"I suggested to give you a ride. I wasn't calculating the distance," he said. "I'm doing what I think a man should do for a woman."

My heart skipped three or four beats before I responded. Somehow I knew deep in my soul that if I could make that connection with him, my troubles would be a thing of the past. As I started toward the door, he said, "No." Then he stepped out comfortably and opened the door. "Queen, the only time a woman should reach out for something is when she is reaching for the world that the king is creating for her," he said.

I knew that the ride to my home would probably be the most memorable and exciting ride that I had ever taken in my life. Like most women, I love to be the center of attention. I kept thinking in the back of my mind that I was going to enjoy every single moment of this three-mile ride, and wherever this ride led me I was open to go. Now ladies, first, keep in mind that I was lonely. I wasn't in a relationship, and I lacked the attention I didn't get as a child growing up. So when I say that I was going to enjoy it that's what I was doing. As he engaged in a conversation with me, he said all the right words at the right times. With every word elevating a woman, he also explained to me that God never created any woman to be alone. He told me how God created a woman and a man to complement each other and that he felt no one should be above the other in a relationship.

Now keep in mind, in America you don't hear much of men elevating women in their conversations, but he was doing it and I was witnessing it. I felt the twinkle and connection of the rosebud bursting in my soul, or some type of birth that was developing as we rode together. Then he said to me, "Why you haven't taken a stand?" I was quite perplexed about what he meant so I blurted out without even thinking and said it wasn't my time. "Now, I really didn't know at the time that this man would be the man to force me to take a stand". When we finally reached my house, he mentioned that he would love to help me in any way that he possibly could if it was OK with me. I was brought up to believe that men have hidden agendas with women. I quickly dismissed that thought in regards to a man of his status. The man beside me was a black man looking like he represented the freshness and the fullness, an image of the coming of God's gift to woman as a man. So he suggested that he would love to take me out to eat lunch the next day.

Ladies, let me summarize the intensity of feeling going through my mind and soul. I felt that my prayers were about to be answered by me meeting this man and he didn't even know it. I felt so damn good at the time that when he got out and opened the door for me I purposely left my purse on the side of the seat to confirm all the attention I was getting from him was genuine—not just some words and leftover crap that was coming from his mouth and that he belonged to some other woman. I'm sure every woman loves attention, but we just want to feel that it's real. Besides, I just wanted to be in his presence and be connected to him. I really wanted to see if there was another woman who would be jealous to see another woman's purse in his car, or see if it would be in place when he picked me up the next day for lunch. So we agreed on a time and in my mind I really wanted to see what time it was with him.

Ladies, you might think it was silly for me to leave my credentials and money in his ride but I was just exercising my faith. And after all, hell, I was broke anyway. So, nothing for nothing leaves nothing—and besides, this man looked like he made millions. So my few dollars, if I had them, wouldn't have mattered anyway. Now, everything that glitters isn't gold and probably only half of this story was generally told. So when he picked me up the next day, I knew at that moment that it was either going to be truth or consequences.

As he walked me to the car, I not only saw my purse in the same place, but my seat was in the same position and the temperature was at the same setting. I knew then that day was in my favor. The gods were smiling on me. Ladies, sometimes we feel a need to know who we are dealing with before the party gets started. That was my little way of finding out whether this divine man had a woman or not in his life. I mean, on a regular basis.

He took me to a nice, extravagant, five-star restaurant. It was surrounded by glass and revolved in the sky while he enchanted me. I think the name of the restaurant was the Polaris. He made me feel like a woman in his presence. He diplomatically displayed his etiquette and his enchantment as we ate and drank and laughed. I felt marvelous, I must say. Not a minute went by that was not accounted for and then he made a phone call in my presence to his traveling agents and told them to book a three-day cruise for us to the Bahamas. He never stopped to ask me was it OK or not, he just took total charge of the situation and made me feel brand new.

I was amazed by his determination and his aggressiveness. But his charming way of setting the mood was yet to come. We left and headed down the glass elevators. The elevator stopped on the eleventh floor. Two men got in and they shook their head at Burt. He responded, "Now or never." They pulled roses from behind their backs and gave them to me. One went on his knees, and the other one sang the song "I Met the Perfect Stranger" by Kem. I felt the moment. I felt our souls start touching in such a way that I never felt before.

As he finished the song, the two white men picked me up as they walked beside Burt. They put me on a carriage as we were driven by two white horses. The women driving gave me full attention and mentioned that Burt had seen something in me that he wanted to help bring alive. Ladies, do I need to say any more?

It went on for months and months of nonstop, eternity-like movements and magical music to my heart. I felt myself being touched by this man so divinely, like never before in this world and not by any other man. As our souls moved Ifelt we knew each other in some time and space that we were unlatching former existence right here on earth. If this man would have said "Jump," I would have said, "How high?" He really had me wrapped around his finger.

I had let my guard down. My heart was opened and my thoughts had been converted to his way, to his world. I felt joy. He was maneuvering me as though I were a chess piece, but I loved every minute of it. This feeling was greater than anything that anybody could have given me. So I thought I left myself open to be a victim of circumstances. He moved on that one door, and kept opening another door to my emotions, my mind, and my way of thinking. I was totally lost in lust, love, and ecstasy.

Chapter 2

I Fell into His Charming Trap of Control

Burt had me so mesmerized over him and his charming ways and the things that he had done for me that I was comfortable with him. Not only did I let down my guard, hell, I let down my heart. When I was around his influential friends and they spoke to me, I had to look at Burt to get his approval because the last thing I wanted to do was make Burt look foolish or unaccepted in their eyes. Burt must have known how I felt because he quickly nodded either acceptance or denial to speak to them. If Burt's gestures looked like he didn't really like the individual, my comments would be cold and short. I guess Burt and I were developing a secret language. Or so I thought, ladies. Was it the beginning of control?

Burt moved so gracefully and aggressively in the presence of his friends and with just a few words you could see his friends giving in to Burt's words. Burt had a way of paving the road, making everything look so easy to me as well as to others. I tell you, he was so articulate with his words and his movements it seemed as if he were being guided by angels. And when you are in the presence of angels, everybody is content with what comes from their mouths. Burt made me feel so comfortable and at ease that I gave up my home to be with him. After all, I wanted to stay in his presence and stay connected to him. I didn't want to live or stay on the other side of townaway from him. So when I suggested to Burt that my mortgage payments were about to escalate because the structure of the loan, he replied so gracefully, as if he already knew. He said to have others pay for it instead of you. His wisdom was so great and far that if he would have told me to lie on my back and roll over three times and crow I would have because I saw no wrong in Burt.

I knew Burt was genuine and a genius when it came to making investments and his wisdom outweighed many men. He told me to get rid of my one house and he would show me how to own more. I knew he could because he owned ten houses. So, taking advice from Burt was acceptable in my heart and head. Ladies, I felt as though I had a guru and a God. Being protected and shielded and loved by God was what I thought I had. I'm sure that's what all women want. By this time, I was extremely comfortable and controlled by Burt. He already had someone picked out to rent my house. He had a woman meet us at my house and Burt showed her all around. Burt explained to her all the things that he would do as far as the repairs—what he would and wouldn't repair. I didn't have to say a word. I didn't need to because I'm sure the woman probably wouldn't have listened to me anyway; Burt had a way of captivating one's attention, so I never let doubt or anything negative come into my mind when Burt was speaking or displaying his wisdom.

The lady liked the house. She was so thrilled that she gave Burt the money without even signing the lease. Burt gave her the keys and told the lady to meet him at his office the next day. Now women, I'm sure if this would have been you, and a beautiful woman who was flirtatious and as ready as the word "go" entertained your man without giving you any acknowledgement, you would have felt a bit jealous. See, but I didn't. Burt had me so under control that I couldn't see that. Oh yes, he was a man of the hour. The young lady reached over and gave Burt a big hug and kiss. I thought that she was just so happy that Burt had given her the house and charged her half of what the monthly mortgage payment was worth, so when she kissed Burt I felt happy for her myself. Then Burt smiled, wrapped his arms around me, and said, "I think we have a good tenant here, don't you?" I felt like the slave in *Coming to America* and said to Burt, "Whatever you want" without hesitation.

Burt also mentioned to the lady if she paid the rent faithfully for such a length of time he would help her own the house. He told her he's just looking for somebody who's going to do right and be loyal to him. He looked over at me and said "Are you ready? Is that right?" Again, I found myself saying, "Whatever you want" as we proceeded to exit. Not one thought entered my mind about this whole ordeal because I always have given Burt the floor to do whatever he wanted. When Burt opened the door for me and got in the car, he kissed me and said, "I am proud of you. You handled yourself so well." I tell you, to hear those words of acceptance coming from Burt, I felt as though I was doing what he wanted me to do without even knowing what I was doing or how it had gotten to that point. But little did I know I had failed to realize that I was being controlled by someone. This is what they consider to be the deepest, darkest degree of control. I was the victim.

Burt kissed my hand and gave me the money the woman had given him for the rent. I didn't even take time to count it; I consciously and subconsciously gave it back to him to do whatever he wanted to do with it. I think it was only two hundred to three hundred dollars, I don't recall. But I do recall that my mortgage note was a thousand dollars a month and that wasn't what she gave him, but who cares? Burt knew what was best for me, I'm sure.

Now ladies, hold on to your wigs and accessories while I tell you what happened after that. Burt got a phone call and I heard the woman say her name was Rita. I didn't pay too much attention or try to put things together at that time but I know the woman said, "I am the Rita that just rented out your house." I heard Burt say in such a joyous way to her, "I like your loyalty so far that I would like to see more. So when you and I sit down and talk, remind me to give you tickets to the Bahamas so I may show you what I would like to do for you for showing your beginning signs of loyalty."

As Burt hung the phone up he came to a stop. A solicitor came to the window and asked us for money. Burt had put the money in the middle of the console of the car. He looked at me and down toward the money. I picked it up and again I was trying to read Burt's expression. Burt showed no expression as he could have been thinking about something else, but I knew that he had left it up to me to decide how much to give the beggar. Because Burt had no expression, I gave all the money to the beggar. Then the light changed. Burt pulled in to Sonic restaurant and ordered. When the waitress brought our food over, Burt looked where the money had been, then looked back at me. I knew then I had made a big, major, stupid, ridiculous, and unacceptable mistake by giving the beggar all the money. But keep in mind I was just trying to keep Burt happy, meet his expectation, and show Burt my good heart. I wanted to show him I was a cheerful giver and money was not the thing with me; Burt was.

Burt quickly paid the waitress and looked at me in such a cold, dark, and evil way that I had never seen in this man before. Then he said to me, "From here out, allow me baby, Deja, to think for you. Allow me to do for you, allow me to make you because I care for you and nobody else could care for you and love you the way I do. So I need you to be in the back of me until I build you up to where I need you to be, so people won't take advantage of you."

Again, I never questioned Burt by that time. I was just so hurt over the mistake and not getting Burt's approval that I was angry with myself. I didn't even realize the abuse, control, and cruel, dogmatic treatment that Burt was imposing on me. Little did I know other entities would spring out from this act that were far worse and dangerous…

Chapter 3

Beyond the Dark Side

When we got home, Burt got a phone call. As he spoke on the phone, I saw Burt motion to his feet, as though they were hurting or something. I wanted to make sure Burt was OK so I started massaging them. I even made a bucket of water for him to put his feet in while he was on the phone. Burt must have been on the phone for a couple of hours. I was doing everything possible to make sure that he was OK. Ladies, at this time I know you think that I could have been a little more aware of the situation. But the truth of the matter is I was caught up emotionally. When you are in love with someone and you give him your heart and your head, and his intentions for you aren't honorable, then you find yourself being secluded into a lonely world or circumstances that you won't share with anyone. You can't find a way out. The more you turn and the more you wiggle, the worse it gets. You lose all reasoning and understanding; you lose yourself.

But back to the story. Burt finally ended the phone call and as we lay down, he kept mentioning to me that he thought Rita had great potential. He thought Rita could become our personal secretary and he asked me what I thought. I said yes because I didn't want to object and make a fool of myself again. Agreeing to Burt didn't leave any room for anything else to be said or for me to explain myself. He suggested that I call Rita the next day and tell her to meet him at one in the afternoon at his office ready to accept an assignment.

I accepted this task without hesitation. When I called the next morning, I explained to Rita that I was calling for Burt and Burt wanted to see her at his office. She thanked me and said that she really appreciated me calling. Rita wanted to know how long I had worked for Burt and whether being loyal would get her foot further in the door with him. I explained to Rita that Mr. Burt is a man of high expectations and if she obeyed Burt's instructions, he would see her through and fulfill her wishes as long as they were in line with Burt's wishes. She thanked me again and said she was not going to be like me but better then me. Now ladies, again, I was so torn up and controlled that I didn't even tell this woman about our circumstances—that I wasn't his worker but his woman.

Anyway, a knock on the door came after I hung the phone up. It was the neighbor letting me know that part of his tree had fallen on Burt's cable wire. I thanked him, then he asked me if he could use the phone. I didn't see anything wrong with it so I said yes. When he came in, I pointed to the phone without even thinking about it. It was located in our bedroom. As he explained to the cable company what had happened, he motioned to me as if something was on his back. He turned around and lifted his shirt up. By that time, the garage door opened and a car pulled in. Burt got out. I was trying to explain to Burt as he was coming in that the neighbor had come in and was using the phone. Burt was on his cell phone at the time not realizing that it was an awkward situation for anyone to grasp. Burt looked at the neighbor, and then looked back at me, and the man ran out the door. I didn't know exactly how this was about to go down, but I know it would be unusual and different. When

I looked at Burt my eyes fell and for the first time felt like killing myself. I was unable to explain because I didn't want to be looked at differently. Even with the truth, I felt I had made the worst of all mistakes.

Burt's words to me were, "How could you do me like this, you damn harlot, a man who loves you so much so wrong?" And I said, "Burt—" His countenance changed. For the first time I heard profanity. "You lousy whore, bitch, you no-good, low-life daughter of a jezebel! You are so low down that God's hands are against you, you tramp. You are not fit to be a woman nor an image. Just get the hell out of my face and go in another room until I cool down and find out what to do with you because to keep a whore like you around I would always have to look around to see what you are up to."

Ladies, about this time in my life I felt as though I really disgraced myself and all other women of the world because the man that I cared, loved, and trusted so much now saw me as a creature and not a woman of God. So Burt went in his room. I grabbed all I could. I had no family, no one near whom I could trust. So I ran to the only place I knew and that was a shelter.

I had known Burt for about five years and lived with him for about two years. I had given up everything I owned for him to make sure that he was happy. Now I found myself running to a place where I might find peace and respect. I ran from shelter to shelter for the next five months. Little did I know that this would be the beginning of a long awaited time of confusion.

Chapter 4

A Journey of Confusion

It never entered into my mind how our relationship had arrived at this point. The only thing I truly wanted was to forget that what had transpired. My stay in the shelter became so bleak that each time someone spoke to me, all I could recall was me running and having nowhere and nobody to support me. After all, Burt had made sure that all my communication and possible friends had been washed away. Believe it or not, ladies, I felt as though I needed to make it right with him. I wanted just one more chance so he could see that it was just not me. I didn't know how to do it. I kept calling his cell phone and all I would get was his answering machine. I was afraid to leave a message, so I just remained silent until after the beep. Ladies, I tell you that at this point of my life I was confused as hell. My down looked up and my up looked down. My days became nights and my nights became days. It felt like my life was closing in without Burt. Believe it or not, ladies, what I'm trying to tell you is when you develop a bond with someone and you put your all into him, it becomes so hard to step away. I mean, even if you had a tow truck to tow you away for your own safety, you probably wouldn't go because a bond is not easily broken. I'm sure some of you ladies are saying right now that I may have been a fool. That's true. I was and I'm sure a lot of women have been through similar circumstances and were damn fools too.

Now, back to the story. I finally got a hold of Burt. I tried to explain to him that I had nothing in common with the neighbor, that it was a sheer coincidence and that I would never step out of our relationship because I loved him so much. Burt quietly listened on the phone. He asked me a question: "How much do you love me?" Words couldn't explain how much I loved Burt, what he had done for me in my life, and how he cared and gave me attention. That's what I always wanted from a man, I thought. Burt told me that he forgave me and that he wanted to work it out. But there were a few minor things that he wanted me to do before I came back. I didn't care what it was. All I wanted to do was be back with Burt. As I look back on that episode, I now believe Burt knew that, but never let on.

Burt met me and I was so damn happy to see him that I started crying as he hugged me. Then he reminded me with his words as he embraced me. He said things had to be a little different. I said OK, then he told me that he didn't want me to speak to anyone and was not to be in the same room with them. He also said people would try to bring him down through me because I was naïve and the weakest link. He said that they would do it and I wouldn't even know what was going on. He reassured me that I was the only one and that he loved me. Then he reached over and kissed me and said, "Let's go eat."

What a relief I felt, ladies, being reunited with my man. That was the most joyful feeling in the world and I wasn't going to let anybody come between us again like that. So if it looked like someone was going to approach me when we were together I would just quickly run right up under Burt and make sure that he knew that I wasn't up to anything. When we rode together and people looked at us together too long, I would look down to the floor. If they came near me, I would disappear so they wouldn't end up in my presence. Ladies, I was so damn terrified, tore up, confused, and frightened of my own shadow. People started calling my phone and sending me text messages out of nowhere. It seemed to happen when Burt was around. Burt would look at me and I would try to make sure that Burt knew that I knew nothing about it. So I would call the people right in front of Burt or give Burt the phone to call them. When he would say hello, they either get quiet or the phone would go dead. I knew something was going on that I had no control over; either a ghost was becoming real or creepy things started to occur.

It started happening so much that Burt suggested that I get the number changed or he would give me one of his phones with a different number. But the same thing would happen. Now, to the ordinary person, it would seem as though I had a hidden life or that I was some type of dirty slut; or maybe sins of my past were becoming my present. But somehow I knew that the day would come when my true intentions would be revealed to Burt. When that day came, he would have to apologize to me for the way he mistreated and perceived me. I knew that day couldn't be long or far off, but I continued to pray everyday—sometimes three times a day—that God would give me favor over my situation. Burt caught me praying one day and told me that people who prayed out loud were hypocrites. He told me that God wanted only true people to pray to him. That's why he advised them to go in their closet, the secret room, to pray. I didn't want to make Burt think that I was hypocritical, so I suggested to Burt out of fear that he teach me. Burt then with a loud voice rammed my head against the wall. He said, "Don't be a fool!" and as he forced me into the corner and put me into the closet, he taught me how to pray.

He said, "Father, bless Burt and make Burt the man he should be in my life. And as I recited what Burt told me, I felt chills come up in my back. I was afraid. But I did it and Burt knew that I was afraid, so as he pushed my head close to the wall, he said, "You should always ask God to lift your man up in prayer." He said that the Christianity I had been taught by my people was the wrong Christianity. And he told me if it didn't work to bring people out of slavery, it wouldn't work for me now. He also told me that I should change my way of thinking when it came to religion because that's primarily one of the reasons that I was in the condition that I was in. I wanted to believe Burt, so I kindly went and got the Bible and asked Burt to show me. Burt smacked the Bible out of my hand and told me that I should wait for the proper time. He said that God would reveal these things to me. Well, to hear Burt speak about the Bible was very unusual, because the only light in which I ever saw Burt was the worldly kind. So I must admit, it was a change to hear these things come from his mouth—or any man's mouth—when it's pertaining to the goodness and the glory of God. I was taught to be submissive to my man, and to be accepting of everything that was said and showed to me when it came to the Bible.

Burt took me in and out of the Bible in different verses. I was as amazed as to how he knew those scriptures but I was also totally confused as hell. And he made mention of one scripture in the Bible that God is not the author of confusion but of peace. I accepted that and for the rest of the night I remained silent just as a kid would listen to instructions from their parents. By the time the night was over, Burt had me thinking that according to the scriptures, my hair was a disgrace to God and if I wanted to please God I would cut it low or off, as Burt showed it to me in the Bible.

Well, ladies, believe it or not I wanted to please God and that's what I thought I was doing when Burt took the scissors and started cutting my hair. With each string that he cut off, he made me recite that I was denouncing the devil. Now ladies, my mind had been taken from me and replaced by the mind of someone else, but when you are in love with a man who has the key to your heart, you would do anything and everything under the sun to please him. Any lady born would give the man what he wants if she's in love with him. So I know there are some women out there who can bear witness to this.

Now, back to the story. At this time, Burt had fully persuaded me about the Bible and other things, so I found myself being in his hands for whatever. Burt then mentioned to me that he had looked at some numbers in my old cell phone—one, in particular, which just happened to be for Samuel, a man I had dated a short while. I also had gotten pregnant by him, and later received an abortion. Burt told me to call the number and that Samuel had been looking for me because he called one of the numbers.

Chapter 5

My Life on the Line

I called the number, and just as I thought, Samuel answered the phone with a "hello." I didn't know what to say to him, so I hesitated for a moment. Burt said with a strong, masculine voice, "Speak to him and ask him what he's been trying to reach you for." Samuel was trying to respond, but then Burt interrupted. He said, "You lying, low-down woman, you are hiding something." Burt then snatched the phone and I heard Burt saying to Samuel, "Why in the world are you looking for my woman? How long have you been trying to find my woman? Did you know that she belongs to me?" I was so afraid in the back of my mind of what was going to happen that I started kneeling down on my knees to pray. Burt angrily said, "Woman, get up and get in the corner until I'm finished with this phone call."

I did not know what was going to happen once Burt hung up, but I did hear Samuel say, "I just wanted her to know that her best friend Ruby died." Burt then said, "This is not about no damn Ruby because I would have known about Ruby." I also heard Burt threaten Samuel and said if he ever called again that he would kill him and me. I heard Samuel pleading, saying, "Man, it's not about that." Burt just took the liberty and hung the phone up in his face and then walked over to me. I could feel the anger in each step and as he got closer I knew that he probably would rip me apart. So I begged Burt to please let me explain who and why Ruby was so close to Samuel and me. Burt refused to listen. I didn't know how I was going to get him to listen, so I felt the only thing to do was to start pleading for my life that night.

Burt asked me how long I had been cheating on him with Samuel. At that point, I knew Burt was not in his right frame of mind to listen to reasoning. So I quickly tried to shift the conversation to another area in hopes that Burt's anger would decrease. Now readers, again my life seemed like it was about to end. I didn't know which turn to make. I knew that the wrong turn could cost me my life; only God knew. At this time, I wasn't really sure who God was, thanks to Burt's teaching. But I knew that I didn't want to be up under a mad bull. So I dove to the ground as if something were wrong with my stomach. I pretended that I was in severe pain. I looked up in Burt's eyes with tears and I said, "I'm pregnant," thinking that I would get sympathy of Burt. But Burt grabbed my head and kicked me in the back. He continued to beat me until I was weakened and said, "If you are pregnant it's by Samuel, so tell me the truth."

I knew by this time that the lie that I just told wouldn't work. Suddenly, Burt stopped beating me. He said, "I want you to grab a pen and some paper." I didn't know what was going on in Burt's mind, but I did know that he had stopped beating me momentarily and that was better for the moment. I grabbed a pen and paper and he told me to write, "I, Deja, am writing this letter to confess what I have concealed and hid from Burt about the baby being his. I can no longer hold and carry this pain, so I'm killing this child of my own free will and accord in hopes that it will never be found out by anyone, especially Burt. If this letter is discovered, know that I asked for forgiveness from Burt and all the men that could have or would have participated in me getting pregnant. Signed, Deja."

Now I didn't know whether Burt was going to continue to stomp the imaginary fetus out of me or if he was going to kill me. But either way, my hands were in the faith of God. So Burt started to come after me. I started to run and even while running for my life, I still had a deep love for this man. I knew he had an insatiable jealous rage in him that needed to be dealt with. It was totally out of control. As I started running toward the other room, I slipped and ran into a corner beam that caught my side. Blood was gashing from my stomach. For the first time, I looked into Burt's eyes. He gazed at the blood. He said, "I didn't do this, you slipped, you're trying to kill yourself." As he frantically ran around in the room, I cried out, "Burt, get me to the hospital!" Burt picked me up, clothed me, put me in the car, and then he drove me to the hospital.

Chapter 6

My Guardian Angel

At the hospital, Burt said to the nurse, "She's pregnant and she tried to kill the baby and she is about to die now." This was one time in my life where I was stuck as to whether I should tell the truth or just lay in a lie. Burt looked at me as I looked at him. I knew that either way it went, there was going to be more distrust than ever. So I told one of the nurses to get Burt away. She hollered for security. Burt dropped my purse and jacket and clinched on tight to the letter that I wrote and then he ran.

I didn't quite know what God was positioning me for at this time. But I looked at Burt one more time. As he ran in fear, I knew that it would be the last time before I saw him again. I heard the nurse say, "She's going into a coma, we are losing her." And as the nurse grabbed my hand, the nurse said, "I am Ruby and I am here for you, just hold on. God has a purpose for your life. See if God can take you to it. He can take you through it." I then clenched the nurse's hand. She held mine tight, as if we were bonding as blood sisters in the spirit. She started prophesizing to me and said although they slay you, although they persecute you, although they come against you, you shall stand. When she said such words, I felt cold chills run through my body. I heard an angel in my mind saying, "Stand child, stand." The spirit was ministering to me, saying that God would never forsake me; He will be with me and be a very present help in times of trouble. Just hold on as God raises you back up to stand.

The last thing that I could remember was being in the intensive care unit, with all kinds of tubes monitoring me. The reason I knew I was in intensive care was because I heard all the voices around me. But I couldn't respond to them. I guess I could say that I was in a coma. I was dead but living. I guess it was because of God's grace and his mercy as it was shining on me that I was living. As time went by, I heard the nurse say that I had been in a coma for months and that they didn't know if I would come out. They said I was pregnant and couldn't seem to contact any family members.

Now when they said pregnant, in my mind that took me for a loop. I just wondered how all this could be here. My life was being put on hold and a life was trying to come through me. Yet I couldn't respond with the present life now. Women, I guess it's hard for you to imagine what was going on with me right then. I was completely in the bosom with God. I was waiting for Him to give me the green light, either to live or die. Now how can all this be behind an insanely jealous, mad, vicious, deceptive, controlling, obnoxious, fearless man by the name of Burt, who had just walked into my life out of nowhere? All kinds of thoughts and memories were running through my head. Yet I had no control over it. But somehow, I knew that if I were still in the land of the living, God had a purpose for me.

While I was in a coma, angels were ministering to me. First they taught me the meaning of my name. Deja, I learned, means the occurrence of something that has been and still is—formally meaning standing, or still standing. I guess it's fair to say that Deja reflects the past and the present of something to come. The spirits ministered to me about a woman being the burial and the birth giver and the caretaker of life, not only hers but others. So by being Deja I have a purpose in life to care for my own and others as a woman. Then the spirits ministered that although adversaries will arrive, they may take you over but not out. I am a woman who has a purpose in life to overcome her difficulties and still stand. The spirits also showed me visions of mountains and at the bottom of the mountain there were seven steps. Each step represents a path to life. If I could successfully climb the seven steps and reach the top of the mountain, I would receive a crown and be able to give advice to other women in terms of overcoming abuse and control, deception, pain. I could help them cultivate and formulate their past experiences into love. Life would then come from love.

It wasn't all that clear to me while I was in that coma. I did hear them say that if she doesn't come through, they would have to take the baby. And then I heard no more.

Ladies, I've heard about women going through pregnancies not knowing that they were pregnant until the last minute, but I've never heard of a woman having a baby while in a coma. I guess there's nothing too hard for God and miracles do happen every day. But have you ever thought about yourself being one of those miracles and telling the world? Well, I was one of those miracles. I can't remember every intricate detail but it was so mysterious the way that it happened. I was not conscious of nurturing my baby while he was in my stomach; that part seems to be missing. I guess the angels took over while I was in a coma and they had a direct communication with my son. I remember at different times I could hear the angels speaking to my son about the qualities of a mother, and about a mother's love and a mother's wisdom. Although I couldn't interact with the angels and my son, I could hear. I tried many of times with the little strength that I had while in the coma to make myself known by interacting with them but I had no success.

God always made it known to me that everything was going to be all right. There were many of times that my relationship with Burt flashed in my head. Most of the time I found myself being submissive and trying to prove Burt wrong about how he felt about me. As I look back on it, I regret some of the things I did to hold that relationship together. For if I had the power now to change things, then I most certainly would do so. Women, when you find yourself in a relationship and you are the underdog all the time in it, then something is wrong with the picture. When you find yourself being a victim of circumstances and finally being accused, physically whipped, and mentally abused, then that relationship is not worth working on or waiting for it to get better. You should immediately stop it no matter what you have invested in it. You need to stop it before you find yourself in a situation like mine, or worse. I know that relationships will have their ups and downs. I'm aware of that. But when it's more down then up, I'm against that. I know that you think I shouldn't have had any love left for Burt while I was in the coma. I guess God was guarding my heart so I don't become a cold, cruel, and bitter woman regarding men. If I became cruel about men, how could I raise a little man for him to be a husband for some woman one day? Many women take this dogmatic approach and hate to interact with men. I don't think that one bad apple spoils the whole bunch. I don't think that one low-down man speaks for the character of all men. I am now finding that every man is judged according to his own action and every man has to answer for his own action. No one man has to answer for the entire race of men's behavior. That's why I hold to this view that one bad apple don't spoil a whole bunch.

I hope you women can agree with me. Now, to women who have been abused and misused like I have, this book and my message is for you. The message is this: We can become mad vigilantes and we can bash and curse every man that we see, and if we are successful there will be no man and no us. See, it takes two to bring forth, not two of the same but two opposites. If we can work on and correct and change the views and the hearts and the wisdom of men—so they can view us as queens, as the emotional creation of women given to mankind by God—then we will have served our purpose. We will have helped a species understand its purpose.

I knew that I had a job before me bearing a child, a son who would become a man one day, and with whom I had to share information about his father. Now ladies, believe it or not, it's important what we share with our children about their parents when they are not around. What we share affects the way they view men and themselves. So we have to be very careful and use a lot of wisdom.

I heard voices belonging to the doctor and the nurse coming to check my vital signs. I wanted to respond to them but I just couldn't. Shortly after they left, I heard the voice of Ruby telling me that everything was all right, that God had me. She then grabbed my left hand and placed her right hand on my heart. She said, "Deja, God showed me you in a dream coming out, but you need to change your course and your involvement." She said, "I would be the one to help you find yourself again." She waited for me to respond but I couldn't do anything. Then I heard a deep voice. It was Burt saying, "Hello baby, I'm waiting on you. You could make it if you want to." Somehow I sensed that Ruby didn't feel comfortable with him being near me. She told Burt that the doctor was going to order restrictions on my visits and that she would let him know when she found out. Burt then gestured with the tone of his voice and Ruby had to ask him to leave. When he left, Ruby grabbed my hand again and said, "God already told me you can hear me. I sense and feel that you don't want this man around you anymore, but I need you to let me know."

I tried all I could to respond to Ruby but it wasn't good enough. She never acknowledged me, and then Ruby made a loud cry to God. She said, "God, let your will be done." I tried everything that I knew to make movements but the only thing that came out was a teardrop from my right eye. Ruby said, "Baby, that's good enough." She pushed the button and called for the doctor. When the doctor came she explained that she felt Burt played a major part in my tragedy. She said she thought that if he continued to come around and visit me, it could be a medical threat. The doctor asked quietly, "Why do you feel this is true?" And I heard Ruby say that she noticed that when he is around, my vital signs weaken and when he is not around everything is OK. The doctor responded that may be true but, it was still not enough for him to restrict Burt's visits. Ruby then cried and pleaded to the doctor that God had shown this to her. The doctor responded politely and said, "I need Deja to somehow indicate that to me." Now I was listening to all that around me but couldn't respond. I heard Ruby cry to me, saying, "Deja you got to make the doctor know that this is true." Then they both looked directly at me and tears started rolling down both of my eyes.

The doctor then made a medical call. He changed my room and restricted all my information to everyone except for Ruby. The doctor said he had never seen anything like this in his entire life. "What you have undergone must have been devastating but you are still holding on and still standing and that's good enough for me," he said.

A few more months went by as I was being monitored and under security. When Burt tried to see me, he was told to see Ruby before he could gain information or visit. When Burt and Ruby did meet face to face, Ruby's first words were that no weapon formed against her shall prosper. Burt angrily declared and demanded the right to see me. Ruby's response was that it would be impossible for him to see me but she advised him that he needed to change his course because God's wrath was against him. Burt said that she should concern herself with her own business. She politely responded, saying that she was only doing the business for the Lord.

Chapter 7

A Miracle Awaits

Days went by before Ruby got a call stating that she needed to rush to my room. When Ruby got to my room, the nurses were getting ready to transport me to the labor and delivery room to take the baby. Hours later I heard the cry of a baby and the nurse announcing that it was a boy. That excitement gave an extra push to my awareness and my eyes opened. The first words I heard came from a woman I believed that I knew long before this day. Her words were, "He's here and you made it through and here you stand." And she then let me look at my son.

I fell in love with the whole idea of being a miracle and having a miracle that I was just so overwhelmed. Ruby said, "God told me to tell you that the fight is over and the victory has been won. He has anointed and appointed you and given you the keys to life." My head went back and I then fell asleep. So much noise was coming to my room. Traffic and all the excitement made me feel like I had given birth in a marathon. All cultures of people were speaking about the miraculous miracle God has done. It was a beautiful sight all around for all eyes to see the goodness and the grace of the Lord, the goodness and the graciousness coming from my son, who God has blessed me with through unseen and unknown mystery.

I was so relieved by the birth. I had so much on my mind. I needed to think about this situation. As I was thinking, I could hear the doctors and the nurses whispering about this miracle that God had allowed, being this beautiful transfiguration of his wonderful creation. I felt like God had lifted me to a higher plane. He had given allowance to me, his new light, the courage and strength to battle the impossible. I heard them in the background finishing and preparing to transfer my Nubian prince to the nursery. There I still pondered on our future. You see, ladies, it wasn't about Burt anymore. He proved that when he abused me. On more than one occasion he was brutal and unfeeling in his actions. Could I love a man such as him? I asked as I lied in this bed. Was it my fault? That put me in this predicament. All I could do was reflect on my life, try to make some sense out of it, and move on. Because, after all, it wasn't just about me or Burt anymore. It was about that six-and-a-half-pound miracle that God used me as a vessel to bring in this world. The world that's full of Dejas and Burts. A world full of confused and lost children who are crying for help. I felt that the Lord had given me a new lease on life, a new turn in my existence, and I couldn't let myself—or, more importantly, my creator—down anymore. I must agree with a famous statement that Dr. Martin Luther King Jr. said: "God does not make mistakes and he does not make junk."

Well, anyway, getting back to the story. It was a new morning and a new day for me. Ruby was off her shift. She wasn't expected to come into work until later in the afternoon. In the morning, the nurses were making their rounds. The nurse who was in my room was named Mrs. Brown. She was a pretty cool person, very laid back, not too old, not matriarchal or impersonal. Her bedside manner was warm, not threatening. Her face was comforting to look at. In fact, most of the nurses were pleasant and helpful. Now the doctors were different. They were stern, rigid, never showing any real human connection. I guess that was their way of not getting involved, a defense mechanism keeping strict professionalism. I told myself, "Self, you are going to move, you are going to show the staff that you are going to get well. And nothing and no one is going to stop me!"

The nurse finished checking my life-support machine, monitoring my vitals and so forth. Once again I tried to move my eyes by shifting them from one side to the other; that was what my brain was signaling, but the harder I tried, the more my body just couldn't respond. I could picture everything in the room: the bed, visitor's chair, IV bottle, the table where the Bible lay inside the top drawer. It was frustrating not to be able to touch or hold my baby! I thought to myself, "I'm a mother now and I can't touch my child, I can't hold feed my baby! I can't caress or nurture my blessing. What should I do Lord? Can you hear me Lord! CAN YOU HEAR ME DEAR FATHER! OH GOD WHAT AM I TO DO! HEAR MY CRY, HEAR MY PRAYERS! PLEASE LORD HELP ME!" And as I lay here, I became more humble to submission. I'm at his mercy. Give me courage and the will to continue. You gave it to your son on Calvary and you shall give it to me. And at this point, something happened. I heard Nurse Brown say, "Did you just move your index finger? Do it again. Can you do it again Miss Deja?" I looked directly at her; tears were swelling up in my eyes. But even after some time I couldn't do it again. But I knew it was God telling me that everything is going to be all right!

Chapter 8

Overcoming My Circumstances

Months went by. I believe it was about two months before we witnessed the miraculous discovery. It was around midnight Ruby entered the room. She greeted me as usual. She was telling me that God is going to make a difference, she could feel it. Afterwards, she quoted a verse from the Bible as she had done since we met. The verse was about the meaning of faith and came from Hebrews 11: Faith is the substance of things hoped for, the evidence of things not seen. She said to me that God had a divine hold on me, and that His purpose would be done in time. By that time, Ruby saw movement. My hands started moving just a little bit. They were flinching. My reflexes were responding to my brain's signal. My eyes started flickering and blinking. She became excited and called another nurse in my room. Once again they asked me to show them some movement. After two minutes once again my hands moved along with my eyes. And before long there was a small group of staff members surrounding my bed.

I still couldn't talk but I knew that the Lord was going to bring me through it. I felt His presence all around me. Now ladies, you are witnessing my accomplishments, my invincibility through my faith. You are seeing where I started from and where I was heading. Besides I'm too stubborn to give up my fight; the devil truly is a liar! So when you get in a situation similar to mine, you must remember one thing: that He is our strength and comforter, that He directs our steps. And we should let Him lead in understanding. In the beginning, fight a good fight. I had to fight for two lives: mine and my infant baby's. Recovery was slow but steady. At this time I was coming out of my coma; I was moved to another room out of intensive care. My room was semiprivate with a television, bathroom, shower, etc. I was still hooked up to a monitor for precautionary measures but overall I was out of dire straits.

I could eat regular foods at this time, but still I had problems talking. Many of my words were slurred and difficult to understand. So to make it easier for others to understand me, they gave me a notebook pad and pen to write with. Ruby didn't visit as much as she used to because of the obvious. My room and ward changed, making it hard for me to keep up with her shift. Even though it became hard for us to meet she still found time on various occasions to check on me. And I was glad; she has been like an angel from heaven to be in my corner and I was very grateful. Ruby as usual sat down in my room and read the Bible, making it easier for me through my trying days. She told me a story about Ruth, a warrior and a real woman soldier of God. She told me about her triumphs and trials. God had made women who were believers of Him. These women would give their lives for Him; she talked about the Samaritan women who talked with Christ and many other women of truth who are in the Bible. I found her to be enlightened and very knowledgeable and I needed that. I needed to rely on her strength in order to fight this demon that tried to engulf my inner being with control. Ruby would comb my hair, talk to me, and treat me more than a regular patient, but a friend and sister in Christ. I felt at ease with this woman giving me allowance to open up. I trusted this woman and I wanted her to sense my aura. After all, she is the one who stood against Burt and his foolishness, which must have hurt his ego. Ruby had the same exact name as my best friend, whom Burt didn't believe passed away. He accused me of cheating with my ex! Oh, I know that made him beside himself. Ruby told me a little story about her abusive husband, whom she thought the world of. She would say, "The sun would not shine any brighter; the night would not be any darker" when it came to this man and her love for him.

He was a tall, dark-skinned man, very muscular, with beautiful chestnut, light brown eyes. She remembered the first time they met. It was at a friend's house. He was the disc jockey at her friend's birthday party. There she was standing in the kitchen talking to her best friend Joanne. This talk six feet two "hunk a chunk" of masculinity walked toward them, commenting on how nice Ruby was dressed. At first she played like she didn't hear him. She did hear him, but she was a lady and her mama always told her never to talk to strangers. But what did Mama know? Besides, what Mama doesn't know won't hurt her!

At first he was a perfect gentleman, as they all are in the beginning. Their courtship lasted about two years. They both had dreams and ambition in the beginning. They were going to get married after high school. She was going to go to nursing school and he was going to be a famous musician. They were going to have children—two at the most—live in a big home and drive a nice car. But of course things didn't sum up to their expectations. They did get married after high school but there were many faults. She became pregnant in her senior year. He had to postpone his plans of pursuing his music career and get a regular 9 to 5 at a popular fast food restaurant. She did have her two kids by the ripe age of twenty; he was still working at a dead-end job taking in less than minimum wages. They had to rely on welfare, living in the project in the slums of Brooklyn, New York. They had no money, no future, just nothing! At this point after two children and one on the way, the relationship started going down south! He became more frustrated and started doing drugs. Nothing heavy; some pot and a little coke, which he also sold for extra money. She recalled one day waking up and doing the laundry. She happened to be going through his pockets and stumbled on a piece of paper that had a strange, unfamiliar name and telephone number scribbled on it. So of course she was curious who this person was—this Sheila person.

So she followed up on it. She called the number and after the second ring a woman answered. At this time, Ruby was quite upset. She wanted to know what connection she had with her husband. The woman was hesitant in talking. She sounded nervous. But Ruby knew, so they hung up. Ruby stared and pondered on her relationship. Her marriage had fallen apart, and she was pregnant again with her third child, seven months exactly. She wanted to call someone from her family whom she hadn't seen in more than three years, but she didn't want to hear "I told you so." She was ashamed and scared because, after all, he had isolated her from her folks. He became not only her lover and provider, but her everything. She depended on him for food, clothing, shelter, etc. You know, ladies, how that is; the man becomes your reason to survive. Yes, I said survive, notice I didn't say live. He possesses your life support of independence. You rely on him to be the man! You believe that he can do no wrong. But in reality he's a mere fallible human being with many flaws.

God tells you that man can't be trusted. So why do we continue to trust man? I can't speak for you but for me I don't want to trust like that anymore. Ruby's epiphany began at the moment of her entering the emergency room. You see, they got in a bad fight whereby he ended up kicking her in the stomach. He told her he didn't want the baby and she "f….up his life." But she was lying on the gurney, fighting for her life and her unborn child's life. She thought, God spared her life but she did lose her unborn baby. At that moment Ruby started living better for herself. She did not allow grief and depression to get the best of her. She knew that there was a stronger path that she had to follow. And so after being released from the hospital, she served him with divorce papers in jail (where he was facing second-degree manslaughter and assault charges). She moved on and started night school, got back in touch with her family, moved out of the projects, and relocated after she finished night school.

Chapter 9

From Victim to Victory

Ruby had new reasoning for living and breathing again; you see, she was more than waiting to exhale. She was really breathing! Ruby became something that God put together, call it karma or coincidence. I knew that she was introduced to me for this reason. We had a connection, a sisterly camaraderie and that's what drew us together. As months went by, we developed such a bond. She wanted me to grasp the impossible through my therapy of emotions, physical, and spiritual. God had empowered me to stand up. We both had people who depended on us so we had to be selfless and reassuring in our actions, a beacon of hope for our families and loved ones. I had to fight for the opportunity to be with them. I was grateful to my mother and family for their help in reaching out to help me and my child.

Ruby was helpful also in contacting my family. They were very concerned, making sure that I recovered from my mishap. They gave me hope and God, oh dear God, have given me more than I think I deserved. He loves unconditionally, the "agape" love I can't imagine myself without. He has brought me through these trials and tribulations and still I stand! I recalled the song that Donny McClurkin sang. The verse goes something like this: when you done all you can you just stand. That to me is the true meaning of being a God-fearing individual and that is where I fling that devil aside and do just like Nike said, Just Do It!

And so as I get more motivated in my therapy, I see myself breaking through these walls, jumping over this hurdle. Some of my days were tougher than others, just trying to reach my goals of functioning normally again. The aspects of normality could be frightening and unsettling. There were times that I became fretful and angry at myself. I will admit because I'm human and I have human frailties, and human imperfections. I have been unsure of my outcomes and how I would be able to continue in my life. But Rome wasn't built in a day, so I've heard.

But I had to continue anyway because I was a woman who was raised up for the occasion. I was an honor student. I graduated in the top 20 out of over 200 students, became the head teller at the First International Bank in Chicago, and after leaving the bank I moved to a small but reputable accounting firm whereby I was promoted to a supervisory position. I was promoted in this job beating out four others, two women and two other minorities. I was the only African American woman to be given this wonderful opportunity. My journey continued in the direction of upward mobility. I was going to win at this battle because after all my name is Deja and my name has meaning. That's why I named my son Daniel. Even though I wasn't capable of naming him, my mother remembered the time I told her that if I ever had a child, especially a boy, I wanted his name to be Daniel. The name is noble, according to the Bible; Daniel was fearless, having faith in God. He wasn't afraid to face the lion's den. His strength and courage was more than met the eye and there's where my faith lies. My son will be a man more than his cowardly father. He won't use manipulation and trickery to get a woman's attention; I'll make sure of that.

Now it was almost a year and my recovery was advancing. I now could speak better through speech therapy. My sessions were about three times a week, two and a half hours a day. At this point I could function fairly well without much supervisory assistance. I also went to physical and occupational therapy. You see, I was very good with numbers before the incident but I needed to exercise my mind again developing the cohesiveness of my cognitive motor skills. This was important to me to go back in the workforce; I was a proud woman who didn't believe in receiving a check, a welfare check. In order for me to gain my rights back in raising my son I had to recover.

I knew that I didn't want anyone else with the exception of my family to raise my precious son, Daniel. Especially his trifling father! Burt was someone who gave me the motivation to recover as well. I never forgot that day in the hospital when he and Ruby got into it. He caused a scene, a ruckus, trying to see me. The trouble he caused was so uncanny, callous, and cold. The man I thought was a decent, loving, sincere, caring man, turned out to be the total opposite. He was a lying, conniving, and cheating man—yes, cheating. I found out later that he was creeping with the so-called tenant, what's her name, and many others. You see ladies, when one is in a coma you basically lay in a prone position, and you subconsciously reflect on everything. In my opinion God allows you to meditate in this state, reflecting on your life and where it's going. Burt was a jealous man mainly because he knew he was not committed to the relationship and so he believed that if he was cheating then why not believe that I was cheating to.. It's mostly reverse psychology; blame the blameless. And I was so naïve and gullible in his torments and insanity. I wanted this relationship maybe because of my past, the dysfunctional nature of my father, who, by the way, abandoned my mother and siblings to fend for ourselves. My mother worked two jobs to maintain her family. Mom at times couldn't take time to bake a cake for my school's bake off. She couldn't go see my sister's performance in the glee club when she was in middle school. Maybe that's why my oldest brother Bruce went to prison for gang-related issues and my sister Tammy ended up pregnant at thirteen and the others just lingered. I just was confused and very lonely. Burt was a charmer and I knew he was good at manipulation. Burt made me feel like a woman I thought, but of course I was wrong. From the beginning I had low self-esteem, letting him cloud my better judgment. He would make statements like, "You're a queen," then turn around and call me a whore, a jezebel, and an ungodly woman. Why did I allow him to do that to me? I knew I was intelligent and sophisticated, a well-rounded individual. What the hell was on my mind? Well anyway, I wasn't going to cry anymore. I was going to pull myself up by the bootstraps, dust myself off as well, and make it happen.

Chapter 10

Picking up the Pieces

It had been approximately a year since the coma, and I continued to recover. The hospital stated that I was almost ready to leave and become an outpatient. This was great news for me, my family, my friends, and even Ruby. They wanted me to continue my therapy session with a visiting physical therapist. I was keeping my three sessions a week, but my lessons were perhaps forty-five minutes to a full hour. My progress was almost miraculous. I was almost on full recovery and ready to face the real world once again. I was functioning, doing people's taxes off the books. I knew I couldn't do this part-time gig as a tax preparer for a long time. I had to leave my mother's house and be my own woman. I had to move on and I did just that.

Daniel, my precious child, was almost three years old. We had a little apartment in a fairly decent neighborhood. Our apartment was decorated moderately, nothing too fancy because after all I had bills and I needed to budget. My money in the bank was limited because of my hospital and therapy bills. Daniel needed new clothes. He seemed to be growing by the day. He had his father's genes, with very big hands to match, but he was still my little miracle—God's gift to me, my recipe to continue on. At this point in time, I took a pay cut in my salary. That was hard for me, but I am a mother who loves her child dearly. I had a bookkeeping job at a local grocery store, where I had worked since leaving my mother's house. The store was a mom-and-pop establishment but I had to do what I had to in order for us to eat. I confess it was hard financially to make ends meet. I had to pinch pennies, quarters, and dimes to survive.

But each time that I thought that I needed to throw the towel in, God showed a different way. I met all my bills—not always on time, but still they were paid by the grace of God. I wondered where Burt was. Did he have any remorse for putting me in this situation? Was he still angry? Was he capable of forgiveness? I just wondered. I even asked God about him. I asked Him for forgiveness: help me Lord to find his way in your grace, your holy arms of comfort. Please, please God you said you would never forsake us nor leave us, oh great creator. Do you know I still loved this man? Check this: I said I still loved him; I didn't say that I was in love with him, because he really didn't love me. He didn't love anyone including himself. His love was misguided and jilted and I really felt sorry for this individual. No good would come to this person as long as he attempted to play with people and their emotions. But I still couldn't stop thinking about him, and so after I put my son to bed, I went on my laptop and searched for his name and telephone number in the yellow pages listing. After the information appeared on my trusty laptop, it took me about fifteen minutes to develop the courage to call him.

As the phone rung, my heart skipped a beat—not out of eagerness to contact him or pick up where we left off. Oh, no, that wasn't it. That's what I told myself in the beginning. Ladies, we all been there when we couldn't shake our bad habit so quickly. We needed just a little more of a push to really let go. So that's where I was—at that edge, that teeter-totter of reality. And besides, we had a child together. A son. A beautiful boy. What man doesn't want to have a son?

So getting back to the call, after the third ring I started losing my nerves. As I was about to hang up, a voice said, "Hello, hello." Of course, I blocked my number because I wasn't sure that he wanted to talk to me. So I put my ear to the receiver, anticipating every waking breath in my body. I said, "Hello, hello Burt…this is Deja." He then said pleasantly, "Hello Deja how are you?" "Fine," I said. He was very surprised to hear my voice. He almost sounded like he cared. He probably was wondering why I didn't press charges against him for assault. But how could I still have feelings for him? He asked me if I were all right whether the baby survived. He said there were times when he wanted to visit me in the hospital but no one would give any further information. He even tried to get in touch with my mother and she too wouldn't give him any information. Everyone treated him badly, making him feel as though he were the reason that I ended up in the hospital. It was he who put me in this coma and jeopardized our child. He asked me what I named the child. I told him his name is Daniel. I explained to him why I named him Daniel and the significance of his birth, and so on. Through the whole conversation he was apologetic, sorrowful in his treatment.

Now ladies, you have to watch it when a man is being apologetic. You have to be careful that he's not trying to get you back in his trap. It's just a temporary fix, meaning baby, I'm sorry. I have changed. I'm not that same man who has hurt you in the past. It's only talk on their part, showing some temporary remorse, because they got out of control and only knew one way to ease their regrets. Nothing to it. But given the chance, he would do it again or worse. You see, this particular type of individual can't help themselves. It's a learned behavior. They've seen their father or male family members do it, so they follow suit. Without proper intervention and counseling, the abuse continues generation to generation.

Burt was a charmer, as I stated earlier. He wanted to know how I was feeling. I told him that I was doing fine. He asked me how long I was in the coma. I told him about a year or so. He also asked who took care of the baby. I told him my family and my mother. He was happy to hear that. He didn't want his son to end up in some stranger's foster care or in an adoption agency. He still was trying to control. I explained to Burt that wasn't going to occur—not while my family had any part in it. He inquired why I didn't want to name our son after him, making him a junior. I told him the truth: my mother named the baby because I still was in a coma at the time of the baby's birth. To me, he was again dismissing what was important to me and grandstanding himself as always. Of course, again as always he changed the subject. If it didn't fit in his mind, it wasn't worth mentioning. So I changed the subject because I was different and wasn't feeling his foolishness. He told me that his mother had passed right after Daniel was born and he was going through some personal issues. He had financial dilemmas and, as a man, he was ashamed to talk about them. That is why he was feeling so insecure and lashed out that day at me. He has regretted it ever since that incident, but he said something strange but also typical of him: he wouldn't have acted like that if I weren't so gullible and clueless to men at times. In other words, what makes me so trusting and not believe that men aren't of deception? I wondered, was he referring about himself when he made that lame statement? Hmmm... he then asked me about the baby. Who did he look like? Did he look like him or me?

Well of course I told him that he looked a lot like him. He laughed; he politely asked could he see the baby, anxiously asking when I would bring the baby over to see him. Now I know what you are saying, ladies: that this man just three years ago accused me of cheating on him and said that I wasn't pregnant. He also accused me of getting pregnant by my ex-boyfriend. You say he has guts even to ask to see my child, the child who's been my source of strength to continue. Yes, he had a lot of nerve. But who am I to judge? That's primarily up to God!

I told him that I would have to think about that and take some time to contemplate the visitation. I didn't want my child not to know his father, but at the same time I didn't want his father to revert back to his old ways, even if he did apologize. I couldn't trust him. I was still very vulnerable and weak. Him seeing me might bring back old buried feelings. He had that magical hold on me. His voice even weakened me. I could almost imagine being in his arms again. I could also smell his favorite cologne by Usher—the bottle I gave him for Christmas a couple years back. He was weakening me at the knees. Hey, after all, it's been a long time since I had a man show some interest. I mean, I met a few men after my recovery, such as Alberto, the young Latin guy who worked the cashier counter at my job. He asked me out but I had been very busy with work, therapy, church choir rehearsals, and the baby; I didn't have time or interest in these men. No, not I; not even an innocent date of drinking a cup of coffee and holding a conversation with a man. I promise I was staying focused on better things in my life.

I kept that promise until I heard his voice. But still I must stand my ground. Help me Lord, keep me from my temptation. Don't allow me to lose my composure because you know what's better for me than I do. Burt tried his best to convince me otherwise, but I didn't fall for the "okie dokie." Never again Burt, never ever again!

Burt sounded a little frustrated that he arrogantly persuaded me to give in. I even discontinued the conversation by saying to him that I heard the baby waking up. He probably wanted his mommy to sleep with him. I told Burt that I would stay in contact with him, not for me but for the baby's sake. I also told him that I accepted his apology and wished him the best. He replied with a statement that followed goodnight sweetheart, have the most soothing, tranquil dreams. He told me that when I'm holding our son in my arms and rocking him back to sleep, just reminisce on that night when we conceived him in our committed, inseparable love and affections. How that night made us feel the very essence of our spiritual journey. My response was yes, he is a beautiful baby, so goodnight, Burt. He said, "Goodnight my ebony princess who is still the sunshine in my life"—and, click.

My nights were long and I longed for a man such as he. I kept saying to myself, he's no good, he's no good. The more I tried to convince myself to ignore my inner emotions, the more I convinced myself the opposite. What was wrong with me? Why couldn't I shake him? I know I'm not glutton for punishment—or am I?

The morning began and I had to get ready for work and take little Danny to daycare. My day started with a shower, brushing my teeth, combing my hair, eating breakfast, and preparing my lunch. After getting Danny ready for this day, I would warm up the car before we headed on our way; this morning was an average morning with the exception of the telephone call. So as I peeked at the caller ID, I saw that it was Burt's telephone number. At first I was hesitant; he must have gotten my number through the listing. The ringing was persistent—just like him. I had no choice. I could have walked out, pretending as though no one was home, but I answered anyway. I answered the call but it wasn't Burt. It was a woman on the other line. She was inquiring who I was and how I knew him. All of this was stated after she introduced herself as Burt's girlfriend.

Well, I was a littleshockedthat he didn't wait long enough to see if I was really going to make it through. Not along with him never mentioning that he was involved with another woman. How disrespectful he was being to her. I felt used again and very cheap. The woman asked kindly for me not to call her home. I thought that he lived there alone; that bastard had moved another woman in. Well, anyway, she told me it wouldn't be necessary for me to get in touch with him anymore. I just told her that I was his ex. I called him to inform him that I was out of my coma and to tell him that I was all right. She didn't sound very surprised or stunned—nothing like me. Apparently she knew of me but I knew nothing of her. How awkward this was. But as a lady that my mama raised me to be, I agreed never to call again. After we hung up, I reflected on today's conversation and yesterday's conversation. It made me sad and disappointed; my hope was up a tiny bit. I was thinking about some things evolving around our estranged relationship. What else could I sum it up to? If there was any hope, he killed it when he took up with another woman. At this point I just wanted out. I had nothing else to say to him. It was a wrap when his girlfriend called me demanding me to leave him alone.

It was late that evening, about six o'clock, when I arrived home from a long day. I had a lot of books and numbers to look over. The fiscal year was ending and the store was getting audited. My job was to keep the penalties reduced. I had to bring home the store's receipts, inventory items list, invoices, etc. My job was to tally up these important notaries trying my best to keep the neighborhood store afloat. Well, before I started working, I had to feed Danny, prepare his bath water, and get my clothes out for the next day. Now, before doing all those other crucial tasks I would listen to my messages. I had one message from Mama, asking when I would have time to visit her because after all, she said, she's not getting any younger. Next message was from my dentist's receptionist, reminding me of my appointment for a checkup and teeth cleaning. Third message was from Ruby, saying hi to Danny and me. She invited us to her church anniversary celebration that night. The fourth message was from Burt saying that he wanted to talk. He said he wanted to explain himself about that person who called earlier. He also explained to her that I'm his son's mother and I have the right to call him at any time. He really didn't finish what he was saying because the machine stopped the recording in the middle of his conversation.

I didn't immediately return his phone call. I went in the kitchen and fixed the baby and me a little something to eat. Afterward, I gave him a bubble bath, put his favorite pajamas on, read him a bedtime story, and then I tucked him in for the night. I then got my clothes out, rolled my hair, checked my email, and then I picked up the telephone to talk to my mother. I chit-chatted with her for a short while. I told her that I had a lot of homework to do, homework that I brought home. I then got off the phone with her and started dialing Burt's number. At the second ring, he answered. Evidently he wasn't far away from the phone. It sounded like before she could say a good hello, he was right there and intervened. It was like the receiver was muffled. I couldn't quite understand. After he told me to hold on, he must have told her to leave while he spoke to me. He said he was glad that I finally returned his telephone call. He asked how my day was and how the baby was doing. He also wanted to explain in detail why his friend called me up and acted so rude toward me by asking me a lot of stupid questions. He promised me that she would never call and disturb me at my house again. I was relieved to hear that. He told me he also went to the store and bought something for Daniel and he was anxious to see him soon.

I just listened and didn't respond to the cheating... Louse. He was trying to reminisce on the past, but I wondered, where was she at? When he was talking to me, was she as naïve as I was? No woman is naïve. Burt was being good old Burt. They say a leopard never lose its spots. When they made this phrase, they had Burt in mind. He went on and on about how he missed me and never stopped thinking about us. His jealousy got the best of him. It always did, he said. He added that I was his one true love.

He told me that he was going to propose to me that week of my accident, but unfortunately he didn't get a chance to. He went to the jewelry department and picked out a white sapphire ring—a five-karat diamond sapphire. His plan was to surprise me when I arrived at the Polaris restaurant. Kneeling in a traditional pose, he was going to sing "This Ring," recorded and sung by the Shalimars. It was going to be a night to remember, and take my breath away. Well, I don't know why he felt that I still would believe what he said. Oh, it was quite the contrary. I hadn't seen him in more than three years, but I'm sure his nose was just like the fictional Walt Disney character; he didn't fool me anymore. He was a liar. I pondered what he really wanted from me. I asked, "Isn't she, your girlfriend, looking for you? Don't you think it's rude to be having a conversation with someone else, especially a woman, while she's waiting on the sidelines? Isn't there any shame in his game?" I felt for her. I remember those times. My feelings didn't mean squat! Nada, zero. I was just someone whom he could bully and control. And for a long time while I lied in my bed, I hated him, myself, and sometimes God for not letting me go when I couldn't do anything but cry because of my helplessness and pitiful life. It made me angry all over again.

So that's why I had to get off the phone with him. I saw the tyrant and dictator who must have control. At this point, I told him that I had brought some of my work home and needed to spend time so some of it would be prepared for the next morning for my employer. And as I looked at my clock that was on my nightstand, I saw the time pushing 10:30 p.m. I needed to concentrate on my work and less on this bullsh-t artist (excuse me, Lord). But of course, Burt had said his slick goodbye, saying all the things that any girl wanted to hear. The way he enunciated his words, his flair and style of reaching a girl's heartstrings was like a poet in motion, a painter painting his masterpiece. I tell you, ladies, he was some piece of work—one of a kind in his species. Billy Dee didn't have anything on him, nor Denzel, or any of these young guys who try to be playas out here. But me, I was finished and through playing the mind games or allowing myself to be played. In my book, it was over and kaput!

Chapter 11

Taking a Stand

I stayed up for another couple of hours burying myself in work, trying to keep myself from thinking about him. Of course, this was temporary; it's the same as putting a small Band-Aid on a big, huge gash. I needed this man like I needed a hole in my head. What was wrong with this picture? Well, remember, I said I had had enough of his foolishness. Well, I lied at least to myself. I think I spoke to him if not every night than every other night. I even e-mailed him to find out how he was doing. Many times I used our baby as an excuse to communicate with him. I know it was lame, but I was desperate, like the housewives on TV. It was shameful and very embarrassing all around.

Once again, he became my bad habit, my drug! But not in a sense on how we use to be; no, this was different. He wanted to be in my life for reasons other than manipulation and control; he needed me to adjust some issues that he was having at his firm. He even told me he would double my salary if I would come to work for him full-time. I explained to him that I had to think about it. I told him that I would get back to him at a later date. I basically had to take this matter to a higher authority; wisdom had settled in before I went further. Nevertheless, the proposal was presented to my commander and chief. I needed guidance in making the right decision that not only would affect my life but also my precious little boy. God knew I needed the money. I could upgrade myself, move away, purchase a better car and even buy a house for my child and me. Ladies, I know what you are saying, why don't I sue him for child support and be done with it? But he knew that wasn't me. I like earning my money, being independent. I was not waiting for a check every two weeks for me to take care of my responsibilities, or waiting for assistance from the system. That's not me. Maybe others are fine with that, but not me.

Burt knew this would be a way to bring me out of the flames, along with seeing me and our son more often. And for a while it worked. I took up his offer with a few minor conditions this was to be strictly a business collaboration, meaning no strings attached. I must have access to all company files, including the classified ones. I wanted a company car to drive, fully loaded of course, four weeks of paid vacation time and a grantee pension when I retire. I wanted all this in writing so that my attorney could look over my contract. Burt was annoyed at my proposal, but he simultaneously respected my business offer. I didn't pull any punches. I went right for the chase. I decided if I was going back to work with the big boys, I needed to start thinking like one.

Burt agreed to all my terms except allowing access to the classified documents. I thought, what was he hiding? Why was he being so secretive? And it couldn't be good because he kept all his important documents in his safe under lock and key; only he knew the combination. But what did I know, or care to know? I had a full-time job. I didn't care how I got the job; I just had it. Everything was finally falling into place. Well, so I thought! Months went by without any problems. I was doing accounting, figuring out some things that weren't quite leveling out. There were missing receipts, credit cards were used for strange, unfamiliar entertainment purposes, and employee names were used more than once for the same items. And ex-employees who left the firm months and years ago were still on the rosters. I saw many discrepancies and many red flags I'm not surprised he ran his firm like he ran his life; it looks good from the outside but when you get down to it, the core, the meat of the animal, you see it's filled with parasites and decay.

I knew it was a matter of time before the bottom fell out. Chaotic, cataclysmic disaster was waiting in the wings. I don't know if Burt was fully aware of what was happening at his business. Or was he involved in this, directly or indirectly? Something was about to happen, and very soon. My personal involvement had nothing to do with my professionalism; I was grounded and prepared, fixated on cleaning up this paperwork because, after all, he owed me. I deserved my dignity and integrity as a woman and as a Nubian queen. From the time he met me, he won my heart by making constant alterations in the fabric of my mind, soul, and spirit. For a long time, I was captured by evil, dogmatic brainwashing. I felt idiotic, dumbfounded, worthless, and merely stupid; there wasn't a day that didn't go by that Burt wasn't constantly badgering me. He said that he was trying to strengthen me, but I knew better. It didn't make me feel good. His ridicule and negative criticism didn't lead me to freedom; rather, it led me to condescending condemnation. He is just a very mean man! Every time I think he has sincerity, an inkling of my heart, he would always prove me wrong. Burt was a creep and he was not going to change. The only thing that I could do for him was pray that God showed mercy.

I revealed Burt's finances for a reason. I basically was to straighten out his messy finances; God used him to bring forth a better me, a wiser woman who could stand the test of time. God will make your enemies your footstool and that's exactly what God did. Burt became my footstool; no weapon formed against me shall prosper. I guess he had to trust me because he couldn't trust too many other people. I knew that he really trusted his business partners. As for his trifling family, all they knew how to do was beg. The young woman he lived with didn't seem too knowledgeable about business and finances, at least, that's what I gathered from the few times I spoke to her, including the times I met her at the office. She was another notch in his belt, a pretty face and body but limited intelligence. I saw that she sported a big diamond ring, about five carats, with a blue sapphire diamond. Hum, I wonder if that was the ring that he claimed he originally bought for me. Well, it might not be too bad. He might need that ring for collateral, if it's paid for, or she may need it to get out of town quickly.

For the first time, I noticed he was a little nervous. It was time for the books to be looked at and examined with a fine-toothed comb. He and his partners wanted everything in its place—the I's dotted and the T's crossed. Wow! They wanted a miracle to appear in front of them with God speed. The previous years, they got away with their financial issues. I don't know how they did it, but they did, according to the office grapevine. But this year they weren't as fortunate. The books were looked over not once but twice. The county and the state was suspicious about some of the records. The county ordered some real official specialist to do a surprise audit from the state examiner's department to look more closely at the books. The books were then confiscated for further examination. The Internal Revenue Service was also present; they had a warrant to search the safe where all the classified documents were stored. Well, should I say any more? It was like hot butter on popcorn! Little did I know that I spotted the first problems. My concern was trying to get him out of hot water because after all, he was my son's father. I saw that his partner had a lot of bogus expense invoices to dummy companies that didn't exist or were out of business. I made copies of everything that I thought was valuable, evidential, and so forth. I also made a copy for Burt of all the classified materials. I hope Burt wasn't connected to anything illegal. The office had to be shut down for a while until further notice, meaning we had to go to court—Federal Judiciary Court. Burt and his friends were in scalding hot water. The case was all over the news, including CNN, Eyewitness News Broadcast, and C-Span. You name it and it was on there. To rest his shattered nerves, he started smoking a pack of cigarettes a day. He had also lost some weight. All he could think about was losing his lovely hood, his firm.

I don't think he had ever sweated as much as he did when the government threatened to take his business. Not even when he hurt me and almost caused me to lose my mind, spirit, our baby, and even my life. But I still asked God to show mercy on this poor man, this ill-willed, weak man. Through his stripes I'm healed, thus says the Lord. I witnessed something far greater than me; I witnessed humbleness. I witnessed a man who was weak, with frailties filled with insecurities. God showed me the light. He allowed me to observe closely, showing me that when you are weak in faith there are things that you can not bear. You shouldn't question God's favor, or even make fun of God's children, as he did many times in the past. Forgive him, father; he did not know what he was doing. I had thrown myself mercy on the court.

What a coincidence if you believe in those things. I believe in the divine introspection and intervention. as I prayed for Burt and his company, I also was seeking for His merciful power and to lead His lost sheep in the right direction by redirecting us out of the wilderness. As the hearing began, I testified on Burt's behalf. I explained my job in keeping the books. I explained a few other responsibilities, but they were minor duties. The Feds wanted me to explain my association with Burt. I explained everything, even our son, Daniel. Burt started weeping because he never knew that he hurt me so much. He didn't realize the pain that he had caused me. It was the first time that I saw this man cry. Was God changing his heart? Or was he just scared of man's law and punishment? Only time will tell.

One night early in the week, Burt called me up on the phone. He sounded as though he were crying. I asked him what was wrong. He told me everything about his life—how he had lived his life, and about his lack of commitment in his relationships, even during marriage. Well, that took me for a surprise but I kept on talking to him. He needed to talk and get it off his chest and then he asked me the most enchanting, beautiful question. Would I pray for him? I gasped and said yes, I will pray for you. I started with the Lord's Prayer. I told him to repeat after me and we said, "Our Father who art in heaven, thy kingdom come, thy will be done. Give us our daily bread, forgive our trespass, as our trespass should forgive us. Lead us not in temptation and deliver us from evil, that your glory and mercy be upon us forever and ever Amen."

Afterward, Burt told me something about himself that, I admit, I didn't know. It was about how he was abused as a child by his uncle and his uncle's wife. His mother took ill and was hospitalized. She was stricken with cancer. His uncle was very cruel to him and his sister Loretta. They would take the state check meant for Burt and Loretta and spend it up on their children. He told me one time he wanted these Converse shoes. He begged his uncle for these red-and-white Converse day after day. Finally, his uncle gave in—or Burt thought. The day the check arrived, Burt looked at his uncle and his uncle looked at his wife very ferociously. His uncle glanced back at Burt and told him no! Burt was so devastated that he couldn't believe it. He then went to his room and cried like a baby. His little sister Loretta came in and tried to comfort him. He told her he just wanted those sneakers. His sneakers were so tattered and torn that the soles had holes in them. He had to use cardboard to fill the holes up. He didn't care about the check; he wanted the sneakers.

Loretta lives in another state; she finished college and is in a four-year relationship with her lifemate. You see, Loretta was gang raped by some young girls in a juvenile detention facility when she was thirteen. She was initially charged with shoplifting when she ran away from home for the ninth time. She was sentenced to the facility until her eighteenth birthday.

Burt never confessed any of this to me. My heart went out to him. It explained a lot of his callousness. He told me how he joined a gang and got into some trouble with the law when he was a kid. He really started not caring about anything after his mother's death. He was a pimp and a hustler; that's where he learned how to manipulate women and so forth. Matter of fact, his real first trick was with an older woman around forty years old. Burt was just 16 years old and this woman approached him. He was talking to some of his homeboys on the corner and this chick he called was going inside the grocery store to buy her a pack of cigarettes and an eight ball (forty ounces) of malt liquor. Well anyway, he also stepped inside the store to buy a pack of Now and Laters, a bag of Skittles, a pack of cigarettes, and a blunt cigar. They were both in the line with their items waiting to go through Tran's action. The older lady, whom Burt thought was much younger, started rapping. She introduced herself and he did the same. His homeboy was interested in her friend's girl.

She commented on his looks and asked him if he had ever been with an older woman. Of course he lied because he didn't want to look like a square in front of his homeboys. After they went home with these two freaks, as these boys say, the two women showed them the true meaning of life. That night, I think he said, he made about $70 tax free. The women were eager to oblige these young fellows, showing them the ropes, the methods of handling a woman— especially an older woman.

It makes perfect sense why he is the way he is. He said he was ready to face his consequences. He has made peace with the Lord and if he has to spend some time away in jail, then so be it. I told him that God allowed things to happen for a reason. Many times, we don't know why. I know every time I go through something, I become a new creature. I grow in directions that are unreal. You actually feel your spirit releasing an innermost tranquility of peace. Your testimonies are awesome and inspirational to others. You know God will protect you and He's pleased at your conduct. There's not much you can do at this point but trust him with all your heart. He will lead you to the rest.

I asked Burt, "Do you have a Bible?"

"Yes, I do," he said.

"You need to read second Peter, verse seven, and read the twenty-third Psalms. When I feel it's hopeless and sorrowful, I read those verses. They are uplifting and highly motivating."

"You know something? If I might say, I haven't been a nice man to you, Deja, and for this I do apologize. I just want to know what really happened to us. Why did we fall apart?"

"Well, Burt, I think you and I was only supposed to be together for a season, maybe to bring this child into the world or for us to reconnect with God again. All I know is that He is a way maker; nothing is commanded without His orders. So what I'm saying is that God allowed all this to happen for the purpose of strengthening us. Have you ever heard the saying, whatever doesn't destroy you will make you stronger? You learn from your mistakes. It's harsh reality but it is truth. But as far as us, I don't think it will be us again. Why is it that? Because we hooked up for the wrong reasons and besides, we are notequally yoke. It would be very foolish of us to ever try again. Too much bad blood is between us. You need a woman who can accept your flaws, your childhood issues. You need a patient woman. A woman who can be dedicated to you as a man. I couldn't be that woman because I belong to the Lord. My time is spent with Him and our child."

"Do you get lonely?" Burt asked.

"Of course I do," I responded. "But I have to be strong through fasting and praying. I must be committed to His goodwill and wait for the Lord to send me someone who I can grow old with. At this point in time, God sees I'm not ready. Perhaps later down the line. Boy, that's going to be one lucky man. No, he will be one blessed man. Do you still want to be a part of your son's life?"

"Yes, of course."

"Well, once again it's getting late and I must get some sleep for court tomorrow."

"I too honey. It's really a long day for a brother."

"Well, Burt, I'll see you tomorrow."

"I'll see you too, babe. Sweet dreams."

"Goodnight!" Click.

It was a glorious morning. The sun was shining brighter than usual; the birds were chirping and singing almost as though they were praising God. I was doing my rituals: showering, brushing my teeth, and combing my hair. It was a glorious day. Maybe it was the first time that Burt admitted something to the Lord. They say confession is good for the soul. He sure did shock me when he asked me to pray for him. That touched the very core of my spirit. For the very first time after my accident, I did not see a monster. God! I know you don't make any junk; yours is grade A stamp for approval.

Now ladies, when I said, "I made copies of all the paperwork," well, I started looking through those papers again. I stumbled on one particular signature. This one looked like an old letter that Burt had. This writing was different than the others and it dawned on me that he really doesn't sign his name like that. I compared this letter to the other handwriting and I saw a slight difference in the style of the more recent writings. It started making me feel funny that something was not right, that these other letters had to be forged and carefully signed by his partners. They were made up so gingerly to persuade others, especially the authority, to believe these bogus signatures were his. I wondered. It seemed suspicious.

Well, I had to get little man to daycare. It was time to loosen up some loose ends. When I arrived at the courthouse I saw Burt and his two partners waiting in the lobby. First thing I did was to approach Burt's lawyer. He had the most to lose out of the three. So I pulled his lawyer aside to show him the evidence that I found. I showed him the comparisons. He had a pensive, puzzled expression. What did I just do? Did I just crack the case? Burt's lawyer pulled Burt aside before the hearing started. He was whispering something to Burt, but I could not make out what they were talking about. Afterward, his fifteen-hundred-dollar lawyer huddled around his two partners, expensive lawyers. It was like watching football players. The two partner lawyers briefly spoke to their clients. As I could see, their clients didn't look too happy. They didn't have that same confident look that they had in the past.

The hearing was about to be in session. As I glanced over at Burt while he was talking to his lawyer, I saw something that I haven't seen in a long time: a smile. The judge then entered the courtroom. The lawyers for Burt's partners stood up in the courtroom and asked if they could all approach the bench. After approaching the bench, the judge dropped most of the charges against Burt. Evidently, his partners confessed to embezzlement and forgery. You couldn't hear a pin drop in the courtroom. Burt released a gasp of air; he must have been holding it for the longest time. The judge called for a short break. Burt's lawyer explained to him what would happen next. He told him that he would be fined on restitution because of his partners mishandling of the company's expenses and failure to pay Internal Revenue Service taxes. He would have to pay two years of back taxes approximately, but would receive no jail sentence.

After Burt paid off all his debts, he was sort of broke. He had to file for Chapter 11 and Chapter 13 bankruptcy. He had to downsize his company and change the name to a less prestigious organization. The name was changed to Daniel's Outreach and Family Center. And ladies, oh what was in that safe that the Feds took out as classified information? It was certificates of deposit for my beloved Daniel, which will be mature by the time he reaches the adult age of 21 years.

Chapter 12

Needing that Attention

I guess we women always want attention; maybe we didn't get the attention as children, but we got everything else we wanted as kids (except the attention we needed) until we grew up and got into relationships. At that point, we wanted so much attention from our mates that we tended to do anything for it. We didn't realize that wanting that type of attention could be dangerous. It could cause severe consequences. It could create so many different entities and problems in our lives. We have opened that door. We did not realize opening one door invites others to come in. One problem creates another problem. Then we start to feel that our mates don't love us anymore. . So you go around chasing that love you are not getting. You don't realize that you should first love yourself so you can love others. From my experience, I realize that we don't really know how to love. The Bible states that if one loves and really loves, love is patient and kind. Love is not jealous, it does not brag, and it is not proud. Love is not rude, is not selfish, and does not become angry easily. Love does not remember wrongs done against it. Love is not happy with evil, but happy with the truth. Love patiently accepts all things. It always trusts, always hopes, and always continues strong. Love never ends.

With that in mind, I had to really examine myself. I realized that I didn't love. It was a spirit that came in from that opened door as a child wanting all the attention. So now I think every person in a relationship should examine herself and really seek God's face to know that God's word is real and there is no shortcuts in his word. If it's not backed up by the scripture, then it is not truth.

I'm sharing these things with you because I was operating on false beliefs and in denial about love. I thought that I was in love when really it wasn't love, it was just lust. Now, lust became another invite. I was enjoying the feeling of thinking I was in love. I overlooked the fact that I was being abused, misused, and not appreciated as a queen. See, now I know that, but then I didn't. That's why I sold myself short. Remember the saying, if you knew better you would do better. Now let's examine some of the entities and misfortune that arose out of my relationship with Burt.

I want you to examine them carefully because each entity played a major role that caused me to lose my identity. I cannot pinpoint when in my relationship these entities came forth and caused me to fall deeper and deeper into a well. I guess it's fair to say that the first I thought was love was really lust. Now let's look at lust according to the dictionary. Lust is an inordinate craving for sexual intercourse, often to the point of assuming a self-indulgent, and sometimes violent character. Lust, or an immoderate desire for the flesh of another (outside of matrimony) is considered a sin, or in pure act.

The Bible speaks of lust in several ways:

> Exodus 20:14, 17 states, "Do not commit adultery. Do not covet your neighbor's house. Do not covet your neighbor's wife,

male or female servant, ox or donkey, or anything else your neighbor owns."

Matthew 5:28 states, "But I say, anyone who even looks at a woman with lust in his eyes has already committed adultery with her in his heart."

Job 31:11-12 sums up lust quite nicely: "For lust is a shameful sin, a crime that should be punished. It is a devastating fire that destroys to hell. It would wipe out everything I own."

Lust has its focus pleasing oneself, and it often leads to unwholesome actions to fulfill one's desires with no regard to the consequences. Lust is a possession and greed. The goal of each person who has put his or her faith in Jesus Christ is to become more and more like Him each day. This means putting off the old way of life, of which sin was in control, and conforming one's thoughts and actions to the standard put forth in scripture.

1 Thessalonians 4:7-8 states, "God has called us to be holy, not to live impure lives. Anyone who refuses to live by these rules is not obeying human rules but rejecting God, who gives his holy spirit to you. If you are currently struggling with lust, it is time to come clean before God

and ask for his intervention in your life, so that holiness can be a mark of your life as well."

Being Controlled

Ladies, let no man control you; that is a form of empowerment. I was so lost I thought that by Burt telling me that he loved me, and taking time out with me, that he was the one for me. Now, this relationship was not God sent; it was from my own doing. That's why we need to wait up on God. But I didn't that's why I ended up in a controlling relationship where I was being told what to do or who to talk to, with my phone calls being monitored and so on. Now, I knew something was wrong with that, but at the time I was in too deep. I had nowhere to go. He had made sure that all my resources were cut off so I had no one to call for help. I ended up going from shelter to shelter, looking for support and help, which was of no help. I became so confused at the time that I couldn't even think about what I was doing. I didn't know whom to trust because I felt that no one would even take the time out to listen to me. So ladies, if you are in a relationship where you are being told what to do—with your man taking your phone, making sure you can't go anywhere, and so on—try to get out of it before it gets too out of hand. Don't wait like I did, thinking you can change people. Honey, I'm here to let you know that you can't change people. They have to want to change.

A desire to control can be masked in the guise of an entitled and arrogant belief that "I KNOW WHAT'S BEST FOR YOU (SO YOU NEED TO DO WHAT I SAY)." It can also be hidden in the notion that your partner's controlling attitudes and behaviors are, in fact, really a sign of love and caring for the other person: "I ONLY SAY THESE THINGS TO YOU BECAUSE I LOVE YOU (AND SO YOU NEED TO DO WHAT I WANT YOU TO DO); I AM ONLY TRYING TO TAKE CARE OF YOU BECAUSE YOU ARE NOT CAPABLE OF HELPING OR FIXING YOURSELF."

But these are simply variations on a theme designed to put the controller in charge of the other person in his or her life. Over control is actually a prison for both the person being controlled and the controller. When someone tries to control somebody else, they interfere with that person's ability to develop as a human being and to become the person he or she really wants to be. Over control is always about fear, self-doubt, insecurity, and uncertainty. People who have a strong desire to control others do not feel good about themselves. The controlling person is generally saying to himself or herself, "WHAT WILL HAPPEN IF I LET GO?" Or, "THINGS WILL REALLY FALL APART IF I DON'T CONTINUE TO TRY TO MAINTAIN CONTROL OF THIS SITUATION." These kind of thoughts lead to an obsessive desire to hang on to a belief that we have the right and responsibility to try to control someone else. The more we try to control people and things outside ourselves, the more out of control, frustrated, victimized, and powerless we end up feeling in our lives.

Here are some factors that are related to being over controlled:

Having lower self-esteem
Expecting and even demanding that others do what you want
    them to do and be who you want them to be

Being aggressive and intrusive and invading others' personal space and boundaries

Not caring about how much you are affecting others

Forcing unwanted advice, suggestions, knowledge, and wisdom on others

Interrupting and speaking for and over others

Attempting to be one up in your relationships with others by being condescending and arrogant

Being close-minded and unable or unwilling to see things from others perspectives

Manipulating and being passive-aggressive to get what you desire

Playing the victim and acting helpless, hopeless, and powerless to try to get your way

Using guilt and self-righteousness with others to attempt to get what you want

Using bribes

Shaming or discounting others

Threatening, bullying, and intimidating others

Withholding money, making all the important financial decisions, deciding how money is to be spent

Trying to isolate others to maintain your power over them

Being critical and judgmental about others' ideals, opinions, feelings, wants, and action

Using emotional and/or verbal abuse

Using physical and/or sexual abuse

Lack of Self-Control

I had allowed Burt to violate my personal boundaries by dominating and taking charge of who I was, what I felt, what I thought, and how I acted.

Lower self-esteem

Feeling worthless, inadequate, and incompetent
Lack of self-knowledge
Lack of self-confidence and self-respect
Having difficulty articulating your own values, beliefs, and
    personal goals
Feeling adrift and having little or no focus, purpose, or
    meaning in your life
Being easily influenced and controlled by others and what
    they think and want
Having little self-discipline
Having few clear personal boundaries for yourself
Being passive and unwilling or unable to speak up for you,
    and to set healthy limits with others
Acting helpless, hopeless, and powerless
Stuffing anger, resentment, and other feelings until they
    come out in self-destructive ways
Being people-pleasing and codependent
Allowing others to define who you are and direct what you
    do
Being driven and motivated primarily by guilt, shame, and
    others' expectations of you

Over Control of Self

Being kept too tight on, or who I was, how I expressed myself
and how I experienced my life.

Having lower self-esteem
Feeling tense and anxious much of the time
Having rigid and inflexible personal boundaries
Being tight, constrained, and very careful in how you present
    yourself and interact with others
Avoiding spontaneity and playfulness
Being continually fearful about making mistakes

Being obsessive and compulsive in various aspects of life
(regarding neatness/cleanliness)
Acting overly serious and sober
Being unwilling to take risks, over concerned with the idea of
failing at what you do
Being a perfectionist
Being untrusting, guarded, and unwilling to self-disclose and
to be vulnerable with others
Being close-minded and unable or unwilling to see things
from others' perspectives

Self-Control

This was where I was trying to get to in my life, where I
could make reasonable efforts to maintain control of myself
in my own life and reasonably try to influence others, which
involved sharing power equally, negotiation, and give and
take.

Higher self-esteem
Knowing yourself and experiencing self-confidence and
self-respect
Having personal goals and dreams and actively pursuing
them
Knowing and living your beliefs and values
Being willing to take personal and work-related risks
Maintaining a healthy discipline in your life
Providing yourself with structure and routine in daily living
Having and maintaining clear and healthy boundaries for
yourself (about body, your time, your space)
Having a clear sense of how your words and actions affect
those around you
Feeling empathy, compassion, and caring for others
Being accepting of difference between you and others

Allowing yourself to experience all your emotions

Expressing your feelings openly, respectfully, and appropriately

Being direct, honest, and assertive with your thoughts, ideas, and opinions

Offering guidance and wisdom to others without the expectation that they will necessarily be who you want them to be

Being able to trust others you choose to have in your life and be vulnerable with them when appropriate

Verbal/Emotional Abuse

The joy of the Lord is your strength. Every time I was happy and spoke positively about things in my life, Burt would always find some way to still my joy. He would tell me things such as, "Nobody's going to want you; the only thing you are good for is lying on your back. I am the only one that loves you and puts up with you." I knew better than that but still I felt that I really didn't have anywhere else to go. I thought that I would just ignore his statements, not realizing that they were affecting me all the time. I didn't have anyone really to talk to, so I kept everything in. I just acted like everything was OK. I felt myself always being very sad and depressed. Many days I would just shut myself up in a room and not come out. I knew there was a better life for me, but I just couldn't seem to pull myself together. I would complain to him, letting him know that I deserved better. But he would always show me a side that made me feel hopeless. No matter how strong you think you may be, you find out that you are not. You really need someone to talk to and help you out in this situation. But how can you, when he makes sure you have no contact with anyone? So ladies, please take my advice: if you are in a situation like this, please let someone know and get away from it immediately.

Emotional abuse is as damaging as physical abuse, though it is often harder to recognize and therefore to recover from. Emotional abuse causes long-term self-esteem issues and profound emotional repercussions for the partners of abusers. Abuse typically alternates with declarations of love and statements that the abusers will change, providing a hook to keep the partner in the relationship. Many of the attributes of abusers are documented trauma-based adaptations to childhood emotional, physical, and sexual abuse. Abusers act out of deep-seated shame and feeling of inadequacy. They seek to pull their partner down to make themselves feel better. Just as addictions pass down though generations, abusers often leave their families for a family of choice, then repeat the abusive cycle from the other side. The abused becomes the abuser and so continues the cycles.

Emotional and Psychological Abuse

The aim of emotional and psychological abuse is to chip away your feelings of self-worth and independence. If you're the victim in this type of abuse, you may feel that there is no way out of the relationship, or that without your abuser you have nothing. Emotional abuse includes verbal abuse such as yelling, name-calling, blaming, and shaming. Isolation, intimidation, and controlling behavior also fall under emotional abuse. You may think that physical abuse is far worse than emotional abuse, since physical violence can send you to the hospital and leave you with scars or death. But the scars of emotional abuse are very, very real and they run deep. In fact, emotional abuse can be just as damaging as physical abuse—sometimes even more so. Emotional abuse usually worsens over time, often escalating to physical battery.

Signs of Domestic Abuse
People Who Are Being Abused May:

Seem afraid or anxious to please their partner

Go along with everything their partner says and does
Check in often with their partner to report where they are
and what they're doing
Receive frequent, harassing phone calls from their partner
Talk about their partner's temper, jealousy, or possessiveness

Signs of Physical Violence
People Who Are Being Physically Abused:

Have frequent injuries, with the excuse of accidents
Frequently miss work, school or social occasions, without
explanations
Dress in clothing designed to hide bruises or scars

Warnings of Isolation
People Who Are Being Isolated by the Abuse May:

Be restricted from seeing family and friends
Rarely go out in public without their partner
Have limited access to money, credit card, or the car

The Psychological Warning Signs of Abuse
People Who Are Being Abused May:

Have very low self-esteem, even if they used to be confident
Show major personality changes
Be depressed, anxious, or suicidal

Important Facts

In general, about 80 percent of both court-referred and self-referred men in these (domestic violence) studies exhibited diagnosable psychopathology, typically personality disorder. Estimates of personality disorder in the general population would be more in the 15-20 percent range. As violence becomes more severe and chronic, the likelihood of psychopathology in men approaches 100 percent. According to the Centers for Disease Control, domestic violence is a serious, preventable public health problem affecting more than 32 million Americans, or more than 10 percent of the US population. It's sad that only 10 percent of domestic violence cases are reported.

Please! Please Read!

Now ladies, just imagine being torn to pieces and broke down into nothing. What is a woman to do after this type of abuse? How is she supposed to stand and feel good and full of self-esteem? How can she still be a woman without carrying some deep hatred around her? How can she be productive in the community and in the presence of her peers and hold her head up high, as if it has never happened? How can she present herself so when the masses of people see her, they see a well-put-together, bona fide, extremely blessed woman of high morals, and of extremely good values?

She does it like this: first, she comes to realization that she has been a victim of abuse. In all forms she has endured the test and has become a master in the field of overcoming. She extends her hand to her fellow sisters, no matter what color, creed, or nationality. She pulls them into the safety zone by sharing her experience, by looking at her weakness, and by making an assessment of her new strength that has arisen from it. She is not to partake in this type of act again, and will hold no ill and bitterness in her heart or head. She knows that it is a trick and a plan of the devil that causes man to move unconsciously out of his lower desire and in his ignorance. She continues to show him, teach him, by being compassionate, considerate, and yet not controlled. And she guides him into eternal hands that pull any and everybody who has fallen from grace into an honorable position of *standing*.

Acknowledgement

I would like to give thanks to Almighty God, who is the head of my life and the source of my being. If it weren't for God, who has given me the strength and wisdom to write this book, it wouldn't have been possible.

I would like to acknowledge all the women who have undergone abuse whether it was mental, physical, spiritual, or emotional. I would like to acknowledge those who have survived and those who have not yet found themselves, or their place in the sun, to be able to take a stand as of yet. This book is for you. It is a guide as well as a book of encouragement to show you that any and all things are possible. Through dedication, determination, and God, you shall overcome all obstacles. We would like for you to spread the word and tell a friend about this book. For those who would like to become a part of my motivational ministry, e-mail me at azalealindsey@gmail.com

www.ingramcontent.com/pod-product-compliance
Lightning Source LLC
Chambersburg PA
CBHW020920140626
46545CB00015B/1015